To The Swamp With Mr. McDoogle

Written and Illustrated By:
Marie Whitton

For My Husband
Greg

For My Children
Gregory, Ann-Marie &
Kimberly

For My
Grandchildren

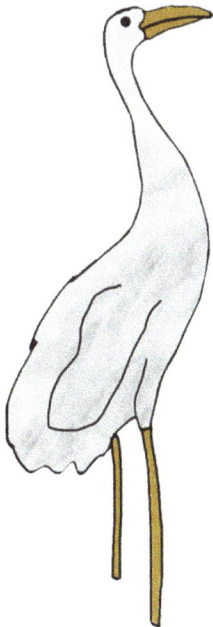

Are there any secrets in this swamp?
I heard that the alligators will
chomp.
Ready to take a tour,
To the swamp's core.

For this trip- it is a perfect day,
Mr. McDoogle will show us the way.
Into his airboat of red,
"We will be flying over water", he said.

Listen closely to the swamp's sound,
It is coming from all around.
Buzzing we do hear from that bee,
and flying we do see.
Chirping of the Crickets,
For this melody - We do not need any tickets.

The air was very muggy,
As well as very buggy.
Flying around are mosquitoes and beetles and
dragon flies,
All soaring into the highs.

Cat-tails were in the bog,
With lots of frogs on the log.
Plenty of turtles, they were snapping,
Look at them, all ready for napping.

Standing so tall and proud were the
heron and crane,
Even in the rain.
Searching for their dinners,
Catching fish - they were winners.

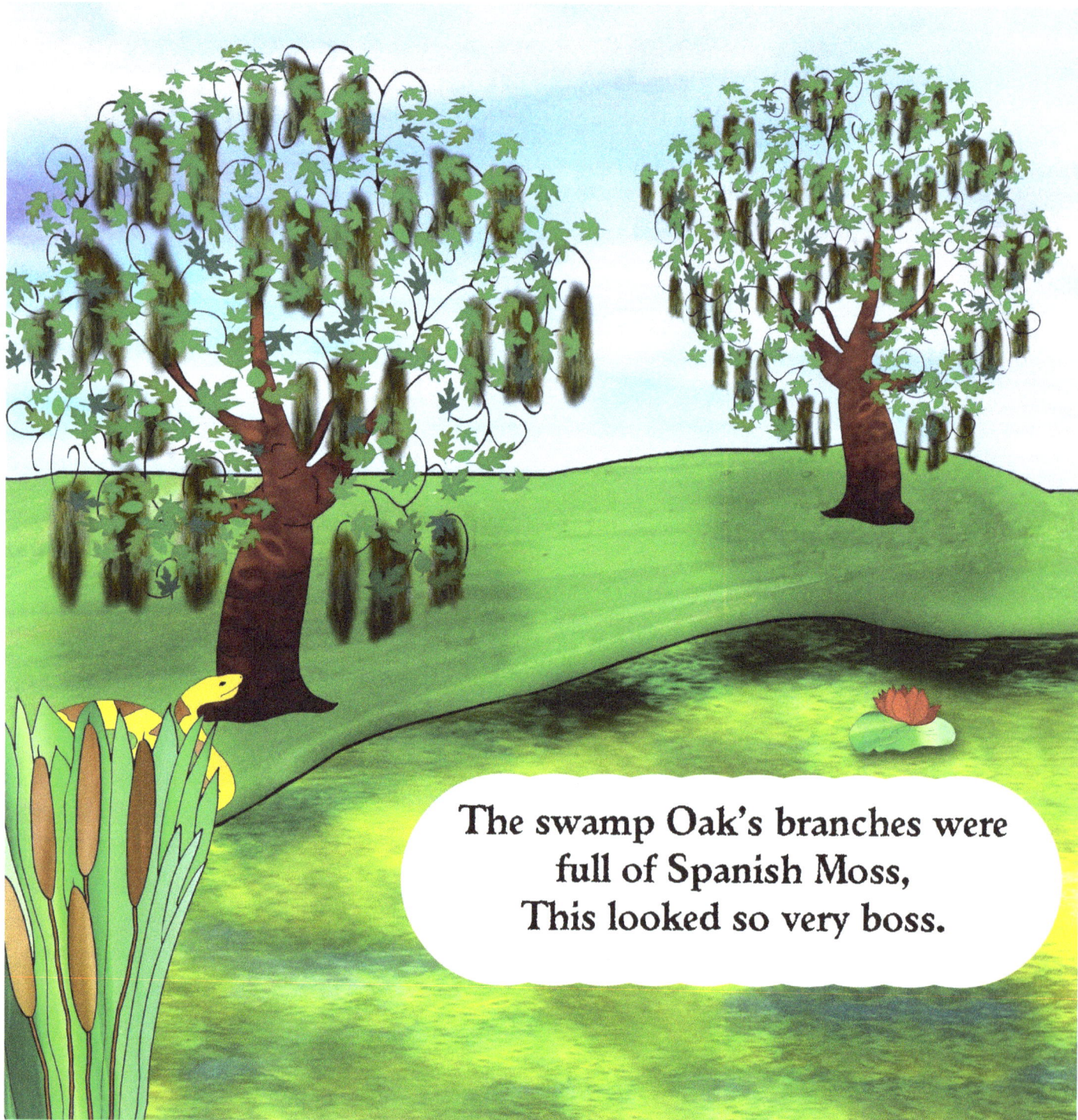

The swamp Oak's branches were
full of Spanish Moss,
This looked so very boss.

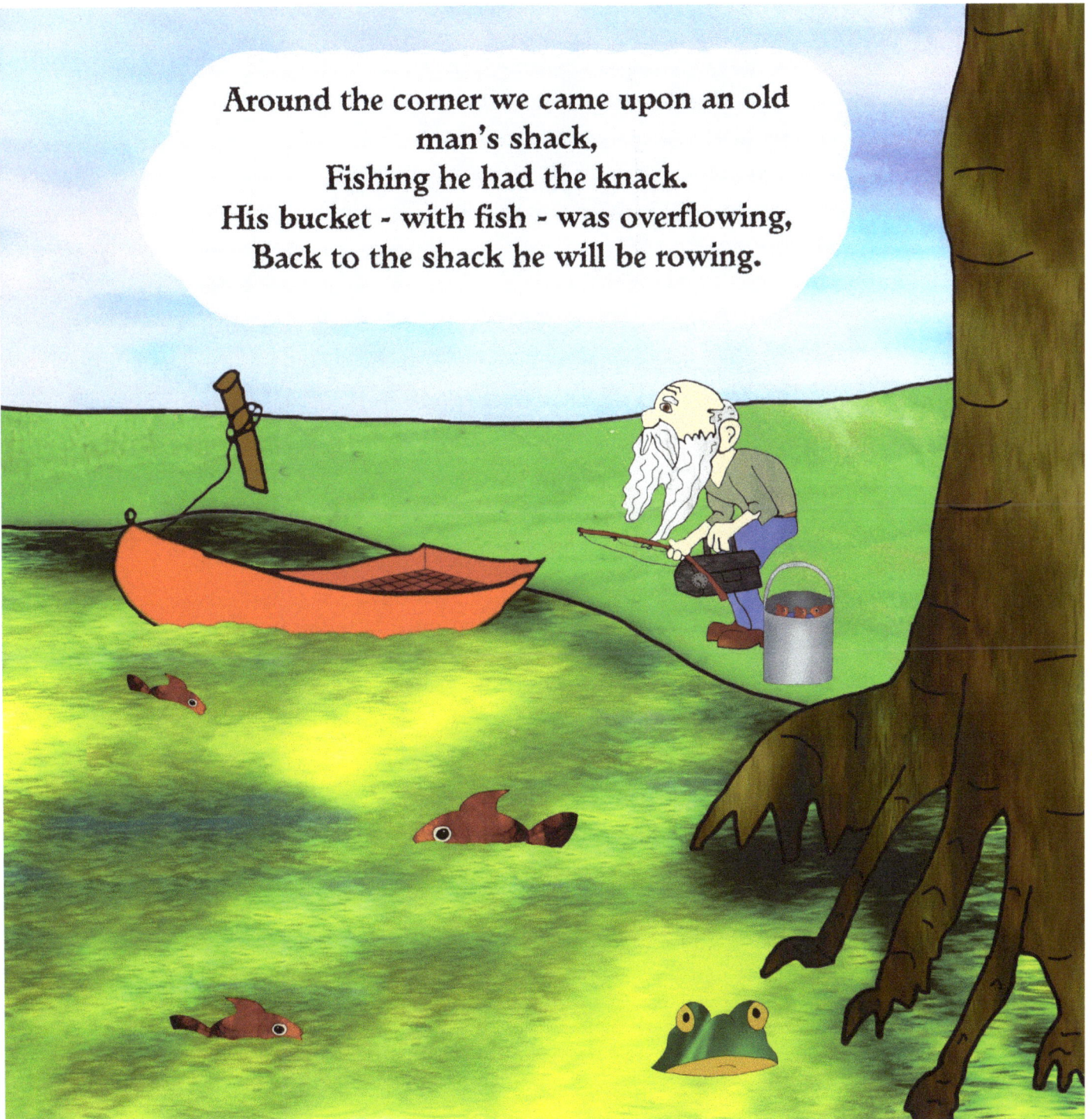

Around the corner we came upon an old
man's shack,
Fishing he had the knack.
His bucket - with fish - was overflowing,
Back to the shack he will be rowing.

Discovering more secrets in this swamp,
The alligators will chomp.
Stay far away,
To the children - Mr. McDoogle did say.

Creeping slowly we came upon a group
of birds.
So quiet - we were not heard.
We had the luck,
To see a group of duck.
The pelicans were fishing,
Looking for food they were wishing.

There are secrets in this swamp.
The alligators did chomp.
Had a wonderful tour,
To the swamp's core.

www.ingramcontent.com/pod-product-compliance
Lightning Source LLC
Chambersburg PA
CBHW060755150426

42811CB00058B/1411